10-Minute Crafts

HALLOWEEN CRAFTS

ANNALEES LIM

WINDMILL BOOKS
New York

Published in 2016 by **Windmill Books**,
an Imprint of Rosen Publishing
29 East 21st Street, New York, NY 10010

Editor: Elizabeth Brent
Craft stylist: Annalees Lim
Designer: Dynamo Ltd
Photographer: Simon Pask, NI Studios

Picture acknowledgements:
All step-by-step craft photography: Simon Pask,
NI Studios; images used throughout for creative
graphics: Shutterstock

Cataloging-in-Publication Data

Lim, Annalees.
Halloween crafts / by Annalees Lim.
p. cm. — (10-minute crafts)
Includes index.
ISBN 978-1-5081-9089-9 (pbk.)
ISBN 978-1-5081-9090-5 (6-pack)
ISBN 978-1-5081-9091-2 (library binding)
1. Halloween decorations — Juvenile literature.
2. Handicraft — Juvenile literature. I. Lim, Annalees.
II. Title.
TT900.H32 L56 2016
745.594'1646—d23

Manufactured in the United States of America
CPSIA Compliance Information: Batch #BW16PK: For Further Information contact
Rosen Publishing, New York, New York at 1-800-237-9932

Contents

Halloween

Halloween is a time of ghouls, ghosts, and spooky goings-on. Get into the spirit of things by getting crafty and making lots of "frightfully" good things! Work your way through all the great projects in this book, creating monster crafts to use as decorations, hangings, and displays.

Each project in this book is easy to follow, and can be made in about 10 minutes. Every craft can be done lots of times, in different ways, using different materials, so there are plenty of ideas to keep you crafting for longer, too.

Pumpkin
pages 10–11

There is a small list of materials you will need for each project but don't feel like you need to stick to this exactly. Try swapping some things that are listed with other materials that you already have at home. Instead of using lots of felt to make the finger puppet on pages 6–7, you could use pieces of scrap fabric to make the body. Or you could use flattened cardboard boxes or cereal packets to make the torch projection on pages 20–21. So before you start shopping for lots of new art supplies, have a look at home and see what can be reused or recycled.

Crafting can be messy, especially if you are using glitter or glue, so make sure you cover all your work surfaces with old newspaper or a plastic tablecloth before you begin. Always wash your hands after you have used glue to keep your works of art from being ruined by sticky fingers, and always ask an adult to help you with scissors or sharp compasses.

Bat hanging:
pages 18-19

Cat lantern:
pages 22-23

Zombie: pages 6-7

Mummy:
pages 14-15

Why wait? Get started and be inspired by these projects to transform your home into the spookiest haunted house in town.

A note about measurements

Measurements are given in U.S. form with metric in parentheses. The metric conversion is rounded to make it easier to measure.

Zombie finger puppet

Bring this scary zombie to life when you put it on your finger, and plan your own zombie attack against other spirits and spooks.

You will need:

- Green, brown, black, white, yellow, and red felt
- Scissors
- Fabric glue

1

Cut two felt rectangles that are large enough to go over your finger, and two smaller rectangles to make the arms.

2

Sandwich the arms inside the two larger rectangles of felt and stick in place using fabric glue.

3

Cut out some features to decorate your zombie. You will need black hair, brown shorts, two green hands, big yellow eyes, and a black mouth.

4

Stick these to the green zombie base using the fabric glue.

5

Cut out lots of blood drops and splatters from the red felt and stick them all over your zombie.

Try making lots of different Halloween finger puppets. You could make werewolves and witches, or cats and bats – there are lots of options to choose from!

Witch's broomstick

Fill your ceiling with a whole cackling crew of these witches, and they'll look like they are soaring away to cast some spells.

1

Cut up two brown pipe cleaners into eight pieces of a similar length. Bunch them together and wrap the ends with another brown pipe cleaner. Leave the other end straight so it looks like the handle of a broomstick.

2

To make the witch's dress, fold a piece of black card stock in half, then cut it in half. With the fold at the top, cut off two small triangles from one of the pieces, then cut a 3/4-inch (2 cm) slit into the top.

3

Stick two googly eyes and some strands of purple wool onto the green pom-pom, to make the witch's head and hair.

4

To make the hat, cut out one circle and one semicircle of black card stock. Fold the semicircle into a cone, snip around the edge, and stick it to the circle. Stick the hat to the head, then decorate the hat and dress with the stickers.

5

Bend a green pipe cleaner onto the broomstick to make the legs, then slide half a purple pipe cleaner through the slit in the dress to make the arms. Glue the dress over the broomstick and the head onto the dress.

Make your witch fly by tying some thin string or invisible thread to the broomstick and hanging it from the ceiling.

Pumpkin patch

Create a collection of playful clay pumpkins to decorate your Halloween table. You can write spooky messages, or the devilish delights you are serving up to your guests, on them.

1

Roll some orange clay into small balls of different sizes. Squish each one slightly between your thumb and forefinger to make them into pumpkin shapes.

2

Use the ruler to make indentations all around the pumpkins.

3

Make small triangles for eyes and a wavy line for a mouth out of the black clay, and press them onto the front of the pumpkins. Use the green clay to make the stems, and press into place.

4

Make small flags out of the toothpicks and strips of colored paper, gluing each flag in place.

5

Press a flag into each pumpkin to make a hole. Bake the clay pumpkins as instructed on the packet, making sure you remove the toothpick flags before you put them in the oven.

Make holes right through each pumpkin using a toothpick to turn them into beads. They can be made into necklaces, bracelets, or key ring charms.

RIP VIP invitation

When your guests receive these great gravestone party invites, they'll be sure to say yes to your ghoulish get-together!

You will need:

- Gray card stock, about 8½ by 11 inch (21.5 × 28 cm)
- Scissors
- A black marker
- A gray pencil
- Orange card stock
- A glue stick
- Green and blue glitter glue

1

Fold the card stock in half and cut along the crease to make two pieces. Fold both pieces in half to make two invites.

2

Take one of the invites and draw an upside down "U" shape onto the top of the card using the marker.

3

Cut around the "U" shape but instead of following the line exactly, make it jagged and uneven.

4

Use the pencil to color in the front of the invite with hatched lines to make it look patchy. Then go around the edges with a black marker.

5

Cut out a pumpkin shape from the orange card stock and stick it to the front of the invite. Add details to the pumpkin using the black marker and then use the green and blue glitter glue to add some moss and the pumpkin's stalk.

Leave the invites plain, without any writing inside, and staple them onto some string to make a spooky decoration.

Paper plate mummy hanging

This spooky hanging is perfect for decorating your house or your classroom. You could hang it in a doorway to welcome your guests to a Halloween party!

1

Staple the plates together as shown, and stick a loop of thread to the back of the top plate to make a hanging.

2

Use the black marker to draw eyes on the middle of the top plate.

3

Cut a sheet of paper into four strips and fold each one up into an accordion.

4

Staple these onto the mummy to make arms and legs. Trim the ends so that they look like hands and feet.

5

Rip the tissue paper into small strips and glue them onto the head and body to look like layers of bandages.

Make a cardboard box tomb for your mummy to hang inside. Decorate the outside with yellow bricks and lots of hieroglyphics.

Spooky candy tree

The noise of the wind passing through the branches of trees can be pretty scary. Create your own haunted woodland scene, complete with spooky faces to hide wrapped candy amongst.

You will need:
- Black paper
- corrugated cardboard about 4 by 6 inches (10 x 15 cm)
- Scissors
- A glue stick
- A toilet paper tube
- Brown paper
- Adhesive tape
- A black pen
- Craft glue
- Small, wrapped candy

1

Glue a piece of black paper onto the corrugated cardboard using the glue stick.

2

Wrap the toilet paper tube in brown paper.

3

Rip more brown paper into 12 thick strips twice as tall as the toilet paper tube. Twist each strip loosely and then stick inside the tube, leaving a short end overlapping at the bottom and a long end at the top.

4

Draw a spooky face onto the front of the tree.

Once all the candy has been eaten from the tree, you can replace them with the scrunched-up wrappers, if they are foil or shiny, or with some rolled-up bits of colorful tissue paper.

5

Splay the short ends of brown paper, put lots of glue on them, and then press them onto the black cardboard base. These are the roots of the tree. Spread the branches out so they look as if they are swaying in the wind. Stick the candy pieces to the branches and scatter them around the roots, ready to serve.

Bat hanging

Bats like to hang around, especially in a large group. Each bat will take you about ten minutes to make, so if you have time, make a whole colony to fly through your classroom or bedroom.

You will need:

- Black and purple wool
- A ruler
- Scissors
- A fork
- A toothpick
- Black felt
- Fabric glue
- Two Popsicle sticks

1

Cut a 6-inch (15 cm) piece of wool and drape it through the middle gap of the fork.

2

Take another piece of wool and wrap it around the fork until you have covered all of the prongs.

18

3

Tie a loose knot around the middle of the fork to hold the wool in place, then slowly remove the wool from the fork. Tie the knot tighter so the wool turns into a pom-pom.

4

Put a toothpick through the middle of the pom-pom. Cut four matching wing shapes out of black felt and glue two onto each side of the pom-pom, sandwiching the toothpick in between. Repeat steps 1-4 to make four more bats.

5

Make the Popsicle sticks into a cross and glue in place. Tie the bats to it using some purple wool.

These mini crafts can also be used as bat brooches.

Just attach a safety pin to the bottom side of a bat and wear it like a badge on your clothing.

Skeleton projection

Dim the lights before you start telling ghost stories, and turn on this terrifying flashlight to make spooky skeleton projections on the wall.

You will need:

- A large flashlight
- Black card stock
- Scissors
- A pencil
- Electrical tape

1

Cut out a piece of black card stock that is slightly bigger than your flashlight face.

2

Fold the piece of card stock in half and draw a long "J" shape in the top section. Make sure the top of the "J" touches the folded edge.

3

Add a set of sharp teeth underneath the "J" starting from the fold.

4

Cut all the shapes out using your scissors.

5

Open out the card stock to reveal your skull cutout. Hold this over the top of your flashlight, and stick it in place using the tape.

Use this technique to help tell spooky tales. Create the main characters of your story and use them to act out the scenes.

Black cat lantern

This lantern might not give off light, but it looks great and won't cast a shadow over your other decorations.

You will need:

- Black card stock, 8½ by 11 inches (21.5 x 28 cm)
- Scissors
- A ruler
- Adhesive tape
- A glue stick
- Yellow stickers
- A black marker

Cut a piece of card stock in half, lengthwise.

Fold one of the pieces in half again, lengthwise, and cut slits at about 3/4-inch (2 cm) intervals all the way along the fold, making sure you don't reach the opposite edge.

3

Open this out, roll it into a tube, and fix in place using tape.

4

Cut a small strip from the rest of the black card stock and glue it to the top of the lantern.

5

Cut a cat's face, a tail, and whiskers out of black card stock. Add black spots to the yellow stickers to make the cat's eyes. Stick all the features onto the lantern.

These lanterns look great as pumpkins too! Just use orange card stock instead of black, add a green handle to the top, and draw on a scary face with a marker.

23

Websites

For web resources related to the subject of this book, go to:
www.windmillbooks.com/weblinks and select this book's title.

Glossary

cackling laughing loudly

colony a group of animals that live very close to one another

ghoul an evil spirit or presence

hieroglyphics a form of writing using pictures, instead of letters

spook a ghost

technique a way of doing something

tomb a chamber or vault for a dead body

werewolf a person who changes into a wolf during a full moon

Index